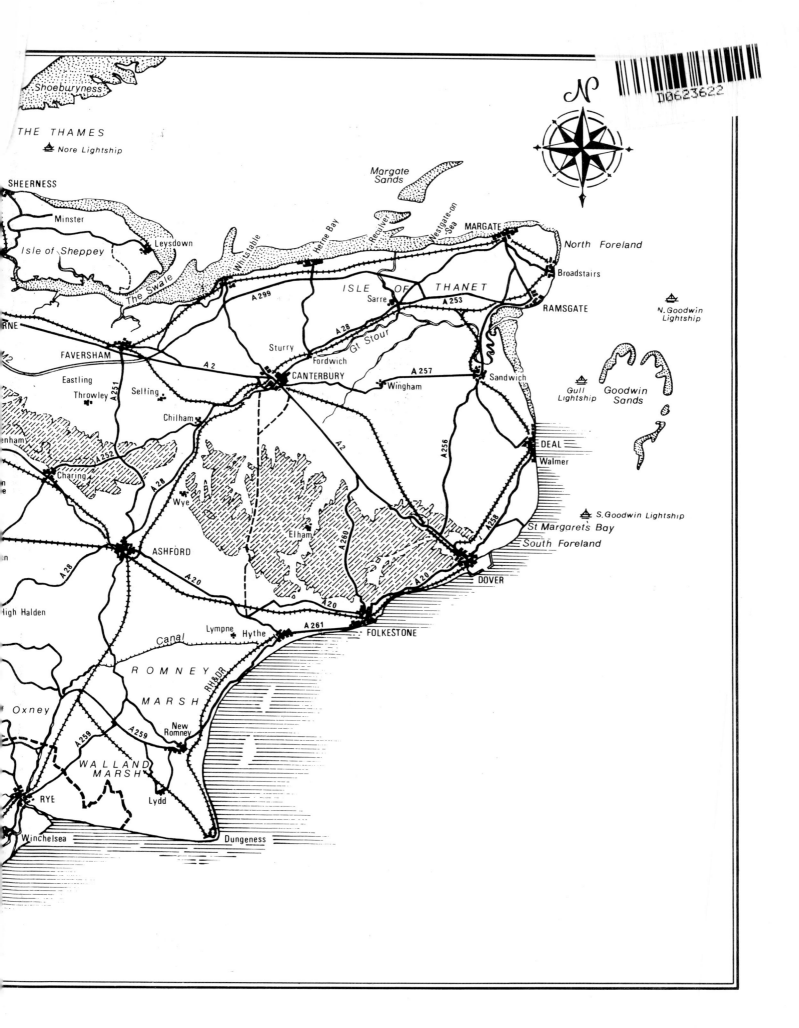

England in Cameracolour
Kent

England in Cameracolour
Kent

Photographs by F. A. H. BLOEMENDAL
Text by ALAN HOLLINGSWORTH

Town & County BOOKS

LONDON
A Member of the Ian Allan Group

Bibliography

Kent
 Richard Church, Robert Hale, 1981
A History of Kent
 Frank W. Jessup, Phillimore, 1978
Kent, The King's England
 Arthur Mee, Hodder & Stoughton, 1942
West Kent and the Weald
 John Newman, The Buildings of England,
 ed Nikolaus Pevsner, Penguin
North East & East Kent
 John Newman, The Buildings of England,
 ed Nikolaus Pevsner, Penguin
Kent
 F. R. Banks, The Penguin Guides,
 Penguin, 1955
Traditional Kent Buildings 1
 Ed Jane Wade, Kent County Council,
 1980
Castles in Kent
 David Waldson Smithers, John Hallewell,
 1980
Houses in the Landscape
 John & Jane Penoyne, Faber, 1978
Portrait of Canterbury
 John Boyle, Robert Hale

First published 1982
Third impression 1986

ISBN 0 86364 031 1

Published by Ian Allan Ltd, Shepperton, Surrey;
and printed in Italy by
Graphische Betriebe Athesia, Bolzano

Introduction

'Kent, sir — everybody knows Kent — apples, cherries, hops and women . . . . .
Charles Dickens, *Pickwick Papers*

Everybody also knows that the county of Kent is the garden of England — and a 'garden is a lovesome thing, God wot'. But there are many kinds of garden and Kent can claim the distinction many times over. A pleasure ground for the quiet contemplation of the works of nature? Who can doubt that parts of Kent are eminently that? A region of careful cultivation and mellow fruitfulness? Apple orchards, cherry orchards, hop-gardens, well-tended farms and sunlit uplands filled with sheep: Kent has them all. A castle garden? A place of undisturbed tranquility and gentle growing things in times of peace, a cockpit of close action when the castle is under siege? Kent is England's barbican, a fortified gateway to an uncertain outside world. And with its saints and its martyrs, its distinctive village churches and its two cathedrals — even its own archbishop — Kent has that other distinction often afforded to gardens of being close to God.

The complex geology of the south-east corner of England has endowed Kent with a variety of underlying rocks which in turn means not only a variety of scenery and soils but also of the things that have their roots in the ground. There is thus a wealth of trees, woodlands, crops, livestock, building materials and the very buildings themselves.

Structurally the south-east region consists of an elongated and eroded dome of sedimentary rock which once lay under some primeval sea. Erosion has removed all the higher parts of the dome and what is left are curved narrow bands around the core of older strata in the centre that make up the feature we call the Weald. The north-west corner of the feature lies in Surrey, Sussex covers the southern half and its northern boundary with Kent runs just to the north and parallel with the crest of the Weald. Kent thus comprises several slightly curved parallel bands of strata running north-west/south-east across the county bounded by the English Channel in the east and the Thames Estuary in the north. In the south along the border with Sussex runs a belt of sandstone about 10 miles wide known as 'Hastings Beds', a hilly area once heavily forested — hence the name Weald — and from the 13th to the early 18th centuries, a centre for iron smelting. The names of the Wealden villages and towns tell their own story with the Old English suffix 'hurst' — a wooded hill — Lamberhurst, Gouldhurst, Hawkhurst, Sissinghurst. The next belt to the north, again about 10 miles wide, is the Wealden Clay. Comparatively cold and wet, it once grew dense forests of oaks which supplied timber for shipbuilding and for the frames of half-timbered houses with which the region abounds. The 'den' endings found in the region — Marden, Biddenden, Bethersden, Tenterden — mean forest clearings for swine pastures. The area is still largely permanent pasture for grazing cattle rather than pigs and a good deal of London's milk comes from the area. North of the clay is a scarp-faced ridge about five miles wide of 'Lower Greensand' running through Sevenoaks, Maidstone and on to Ashford and Folkestone. Underlying sandy heathland west of Maidstone, it forms part of the fruit belt of mid-Kent further east. Parts of it also provide hard bands of sandy limestone known as 'ragstone', a useful building stone.

Between the Greensand and the steep scarp of the North Downs is a narrow belt of gault clay only a mile wide in places. It gives rise to cold and sticky soils usually left as permanent pasture or woodland. Springs and streams from the chalk of the North Downs emerge here and hence the proliferation of Saxon 'ing' endings. In the Medway valley the gault clay is worked for cement making. The North Downs have the usual characteristics of chalk hills — the steep escarpment facing into the Weald, smooth convex slopes and steep-sided river valleys but their extensive cover of 'clay-with flints' makes them more suitable for cultivation than the thinner soiled South Downs in Sussex. The higher parts of the North Downs and the slopes too steep to cultivate are clothed in woodland in a great belt that runs from Chartwell to the Channel. The lower dip slopes grow wheat and root crops with orchards further down still. The great chalk ridge is finally cut off by the sea between Folkestone and Dover where its cliffs are unmistakably and immemorially the white castle walls of England.

The coast of Kent like that of Sussex has seen marked changes in comparatively recent times. Thanet, a chalk outcrop, was in Roman times genuinely an island. A tidal passage, three furlongs (600m) wide called the Wantsum, separated it from the mainland. Two rivers, the Great and Little Stours, once converged and ran into the sea at Stourmouth, now five miles from the sea. The Wantsum channel was used by ships on passage from the Channel to London until the end of the 15th century. Over the centuries a build-up of shingle diverted the navigable channel first south then north and finally cut off the tidal flow into the channel altogether. Thereafter the steady accumulation of river mud filled the Wantsum completely and the Wantsum levels are nowadays intensely cultivated.

The clays of Kent produce the finest bricks in England and have done so for more than 200 years. Most famous are the London 'stocks' — bright yellow or burnt purple — of which so many buildings in the capital are built. They come from the chalky soils of the Thames estuary in the vicinity of Sittingbourne and Faversham. Wealden bricks are brown, red or brindled and the Medway valley — notably Aylesford — produces a distinctive 'white' (pale yellow) brick. Along with bricks go tiles and here Kent's fame goes back to Roman times. Thatch is very rare in Kent and the local tradition is for hipped roofs with great sweeps of tiles often from ridge almost to ground level in the aptly named 'cat-slides'. Tiles are also widely used throughout West Kent for tile-hanging and in a variety of forms, shapes and colours. From the late 17th century onwards the rather leaky infilling of the many timber-framed houses that proliferate in the Wealden area have been weatherproofed — or modernised — by the facing of the upper storey with tiles: square, scallop, fish scale or the brick-like 'mathematicals' in the yellows of Faversham or the reds of Canterbury.

'Kentish Rag' — found in the Lower Greensand belt — is still quarried near Maidstone but in modern times is more often used for metalling roads than in building. It is coarse-textured and brittle and though it tends to crumble with age, it has endured in such ancient structures as Rochester Castle (page 100), Knole (page 10), Westgate (page 64) and Christ Church Gate, Canterbury (page 68) and numerous smaller churches like that at Charing (page 86). Another building stone comes from the higher Weald, a sandstone called Calverley, variegated brown depending on the amount of iron it contains. It was used extensively in Royal Tunbridge Wells and at places like Scotney Castle (page 26). It comes in substantial blocks but can also be split to produce roof tiles. Flint is also used in the building of many houses and churches in the chalky coastal areas of Kent — Margate, Ramsgate, Sandwich, Deal, Dover and Folkestone.

The Weald was once renowned for its oaks and Spanish chestnuts used for the timber framing of Wealden-type houses and similar vernacular buildings which abound in Kent with its tradition of prosperous small farms and estates run by yeoman farmers (all engendered by a form of inheritance called 'gavelkind' which gave equal shares to all a man's surviving sons). The Wealden or Kentish hall house is the acme of this tradition. There is a splendid example in Headcorn Manor (page 90). Another type of similar characteristics — open hall in the centre with two-storey wings at either end, all under a massive tiled and hipped roof dominated by a huge clutch of brick chimneys — is the continuous jetty house like that which was once the home of Ellen Terry at Smallhythe (page 38). In eastern parts of Kent away from the Weald, another form of timber — 'deal', softwood imported since the late 18th century from Scandinavia and taking its name from the port of entry — is a self evident characteristic in the form of weatherboarding. This form of cladding also provided a useful method of proofing timber-framed buildings as an alternative to tile-cladding. Invariably painted white, weatherboarding is more prevalent in Kent than in any other English county, giving a clean crisp elegance to towns and villages where it is the perfect partner to the reds, blacks and yellows of hung tiles and the lovely deep red bricks of Wealden Kent.

The first settlers in Kent's garden left no written records although Stone Age relics and Bronze and Iron Age burials and settlements found around the county indicate that successive waves of settlers came over from Europe in the 2,000 years before the Romans. The last of these settlers, a mixture of Celtic and Teutonic cultures we call 'Ancient Britons', left remnants of their language in the form of place-names. 'Kent' itself is one, so are the names of 'Thanet', 'Lympne', 'Thames' and 'Medway'. Tradition has it that the Ancient Britons opposed the first Roman invasion — Ceasar's reconnaissance in force in 55BC — from the cliff tops of Dover but it seems likely that the Channel winds and tides gave the Romans more trouble. Nonetheless when they came to stay the Romans built fortified camps at Dover, Canterbury, Lympne (page 44), Rochester and Reculver and linked them with superb roads to keep the natives in check. The Romans stayed for 400 years and besides their buildings, they also introduced weaving, tile making, quarrying and iron smelting and laid the foundations of Kent's great agricultural heritage.

By the year 300AD, Saxon raiders were a menace to south-east England and forts were built around the coast to repel them. The whole defence — ships as well as forts — which included the coasts of Sussex and East Anglia as well as of Kent was under the control of a Roman admiral, the 'Count of the Saxon Shore'. Kent's role as a castle garden had begun. When the Romans left it quickly became a cockpit. The legend is that in 449AD a somewhat decadent Romano-British king, Vortigern, invited a pair of Jutish mercenaries, Hengist and Horsa, to help him defend his kingdom, of which Kent was part, against the Saxons. They were to have had Thanet as a reward; they took Kent east of the Medway. Later they settled it, slaying Vortigern at the battle of Aylesford. The Jutes — nobody is really sure who they were or whence they came — left two important legacies to Kent. The first is the distinction between Kentish men and maids — born west of the Medway — and men and maids of Kent, born east of the Medway, a distinction still alive today. The other was the system of 'gavelkind' which helped to lay the foundations of prosperous small yeoman farms.

As everybody knows, the Normans came in 1066AD. They landed in Sussex but William the Conqueror's first destination after his victory at Hastings was Dover — to secure and reinforce the castle. The Normans went on to build some 85 castles in Kent between 1066 and 1100. Most of them were of the wooden motte and bailey type but they were mostly rebuilt in stone in the centuries that followed. More castles were built by Henry VIII — Sandown, Deal (page 54), Walmer and Sandgate. Elizabeth I added more — Upnor (page 102) is one of them. When invasion was next threatened — by Napoleon at the end of the 18th century — castles were obsolete. But strongpoints have never gone out of fashion and a chain of them called Martello towers was built round the invasion coast at places like Hythe (page 46). They came in useful again when Kent became the glacis of the English castle once more in 1940

Kent's religious importance began with St Augustine. He was sent with a band of 40 monks by Pope Gregory to preach the Gospel to the heathen English after the Pope (later a saint himself) had seen some English children in the Rome slave market — 'Not Angles but Angels'. Augustine arrived in 597AD landing at Ebbsfleet on the Wantsum channel. He was later appointed the first archbishop to the English and established his see at Canterbury and later at Rochester. (He was very much a Kentish saint and missionary and not to be confused with an earlier St Augustine (died 430AD) the great teacher who founded the celebrated monastic order that bears his name and left us that immortal prayer — 'Give me chastity and continence — but not yet'.) Canterbury Cathedral became one of the greatest places of pilgrimage in all Europe following the murder there in 1170 of Archbishop Thomas à Becket — and continued to be so for nearly 400 years. The original 'Pilgrims' Way' followed by the pilgrims in Chaucer's *Canterbury Tales* was probably the Roman Watling Street from London through Rochester. The title today is carried by another pathway of much earlier origin that runs along the lower slopes of the North Downs escarpment from Otford over the gaps made in the Downs by the rivers Darenth and Medway and then turns up the Stour valley to Canterbury at Boughton Lees. Along its length it commands magnificent views of Kentish scenery. We also get the word 'canter' — an easy gallop — from a 'Canterbury Pace' which suggests that an unhurried enjoyment of the Kentish scene was at least part of the pleasure of pilgrimage. In that sense, this book is a photographic pilgrimage and its pleasure too is intended to be enjoyed at leisure.

Alan Hollingsworth

The Rose Walk, Chartwell, Westerham. Winston Churchill is said to have acquired Chartwell in 1922 largely for its wooded North Downs setting, its clear spring and its superb view over the Weald. Chartwell itself was a Victorian house with few pretensions to architectural distinction and it was almost completely rebuilt in 1923 for the Churchills by Philip Tilden — as John Newman drily observes 'in dull red brick and an odd undecided style'. But Churchill loved it and lived here for 40 years and in 1945 an anonymous group of his friends bought it and gave it to the National Trust. Sir Winston for his part continued to live in the house — here he wrote many of his celebrated histories — only leaving it shortly before his death. He left behind enough memories and mementoes to make Chartwell almost a national shrine. But the garden was the private preserve of Lady Churchill and she was responsible for its simple intimacy and cool colour — she loved massed white geraniums, white tulips and familiar unpretentious plants like potentillas, fuchsias and lavender. The rose walk seen here, alas not in full bloom, is the Golden Rose Walk. Flanked by beech hedges it has 32 yellow and gold roses species — given by the Churchill children to their parents on their golden wedding in 1958. The sundial in the centre of the rose walk marks the grave of a dove given to Lady Churchill when she visited Bali in 1936 which lived happily at Chartwell for some time. Around the plinth is written:

It does not do to wander
Too far from sober men,
But there's an island yonder
I think of it again.

Knole, Sevenoaks. 'A palace fit for the Primate of England' and one of the largest private houses in England, Knole was built by an Archbishop of Canterbury, Thomas Bourchier, between 1456 and 1464 on the site of a rough medieval manor house. It remained a retreat for bishops until, at the Dissolution in 1538, King Henry VIII obliged Archbishop Cranmer to 'deliver his house up into the King's hands'. In 1556 Queen Elizabeth I gave Knole to one of her cousins, the politician and poet Thomas Sackville, 1st Earl of Dorset. He extended the property further in 1603-08. Two of his innovations were the fireplace in the great chamber which is said to resemble a high altar and the ornamental great staircase which was later emulated in large houses all over England. Knole remained in the hands of the Sackville family for the next ten generations until it was handed over to the National Trust in 1946. Knole takes its name from the rounded hill or knoll over which its four acres of turretted, battlemented, gabled and chimneyed ragstone buildings sprawl like a fortified medieval town. Its gardens cover 25 acres enclosed in a wall a mile long. The park from which the photograph was taken is 900 acres in extent. Its trees are ancient and celebrated and it is said that some of them sheltered the knights and barons of the Plantagenets. Visible here are the shaped gables of the north end of the outer west face of the Green Court. The gables date from about 1605 but the court itself probably goes back to the time of Henry VIII. Beyond the gables can be seen the battlements of Bourchier's Tower — the gatehouse to the Stone Court. Behind the gatehouse towers is the mid-18th century clock tower built to carry the lantern which was on the original hall.

Internally, Knole has, as Thomas Sackville is said to have boasted, 'one room for every day of the year'. It also contains a wealth of elaborate plasterwork, elegant marbling and superb decoration as well as the furniture, sculpture, paintings and artefacts of its ten generations. It is open to the public several days each week from April to November.

Virginia Woolf (who fell in love with Knole and one of its daughters, Vita Sackville, West) wrote of the house in *Orlando* (1928):

'It looked a town rather than a house, but a town built not hither and thither, as this man wished or that, but circumspectly by a single architect with one idea in his head.'

10

Ightham Mote, near Sevenoaks. This splendid example of the small medieval manor house is one of the most authentic and intact in Kent if not in all England. It belongs to the era when the necessity for fortification was declining and the embattled gatehouse and the moat are more for effect than defence although the latter at least dates back to a less secure age than 1480 when the entrance was built. Much of the early part of the house including its celebrated great hall with an original wood ceiling go back to the early 14th century. Ightham Mote — its name derives from the Anglo-Saxon word meaning a 'meeting place' — has been in almost continuous occupation since it was built in 1340. Its first known owner was Sir Thomas Cawne; in the 15th century it belonged to the Hauts who both lost and regained it in successive generations. It passed to the Selbys in the 16th century and a stone panel on the tower bears their arms. One of the family, Dame Dorothy Selby (1611-38), deciphered an anonymous letter which hinted of 'a terrible blow' soon to fall on Parliament and thus unveiled the Gunpowder Plot in 1605.

We are looking here at the west and south fronts of the house. The west front is built entirely of ragstone and has several 14th century features like some of the window shapes and the entrance arch. The brick parapet is a 16th or 17th century addition. On the south front note the stone gable with its elaborate brick chimney stack, the jettied timber-framed upper storey, and finally, on the right the stack of seven brick chimneys above the kitchen.

Castle Gatehouse, Tonbridge. Unlike its near neighbours and namesake, Tunbridge Wells, Tonbridge has its origins deep in medieval history when the town grew up by a ford over the River Medway. In 1070 the Normans built a massive castle to protect the ford and maintain a dominating presence over the townspeople. The original castle was of the typical Norman motte and bailey — an earth mound topped by a wooden tower with an enclosure, ditch and palisade. (At Tonbridge the original motte still survives.) The fortifications were strengthened between 1220 and 1240 when a circular sandstone keep, now a mere stump, and this massive gatehouse were built. The material used was fine-grained Wealden sandstone which was often quarried in blocks of massive size as can be seen in the photograph. The construction is known as ashlar — blocks laid evenly with light squared faces. What is unusual about the gatehouse is that it was used for residential purposes and had a great hall on its top floor. Even in its ruined state it still shows evidence of its former strength — the moat, now filled in, lies before it and was once spanned by a draw-bridge; it is liberally supplied with arrow slits through its immensely thick walls, its windows are small and it once had two portcullises and suitable delivery holes for molten lead and boiling oil.

The original owners of the castle were the Clares, a powerful medieval family who, among other things, founded Clare College at Cambridge. The last of the Clares died at Bannockburn in 1314 and the castle passed to the Earls and Dukes of Buckingham. The third duke was beheaded for treason by Henry VIII in 1521 and the castle was forfeited to the Crown. It was, inevitably, 'slighted' by the Parliamentarians in 1646 and then fell steadily into decay.

The building flanking the tower was built in 1793 and is now municipal offices.

14

Chiddingstone. This row of 16th and 17th century houses facing the church make Chiddingstone one of the most attractive and characteristically Kentish hamlets in a county well-blessed with beautiful villages and traditional buildings. The village takes its name from a large sandstone rock in the grounds of the nearby castle known as the 'Chiding Stone' and local people like to think that it may have been used for some unspecified Druidic judgement rite. The 'castle' is in fact a late 17th century hip-roofed house which was 'castellated' in c1805 and then dubbed castle. For centuries it was the seat of the Streatfeilds who held the manor from 1598 until 1936. One of them, Thomas Streatfeild, devoted 50 years creating a monumental illustrated history of Kent. On the very eve of launching it he was struck down with paralysis.

The church here is St Mary and its pinnacled tower dates back to the 14th century and boasts one of the best collections of stone heads in Kent — 'a comical group of weird and merry men' as Mee puts it. The timber-framed house opposite is owned by the National Trust and is a splendidly preserved example of the Kentish vernacular, 16th century in origin. Particular points to note are the steeply pitched tiled roof and the steep gables which are jettied (overhanging). The centre gable is carried forward to form a perch supported by oak pillars; the gable on the right has an oriel window just visible behind the roof of the lychgate. Also of interest is the massive brick chimney stack forward of the ridge — once the position, perhaps, of the original roof vent of the open hearth fire. Notice too the mullioned and transomed windows.

Groombridge Place. Almost astride the Kent-Sussex border, its moat watered by the stream that divides the two counties, Groombridge Place has a history that goes back to the time of Henry V. At that time the manor was held by Sir Richard Waller who captured the Duke of Orleans, father of Louis XII at Agincourt in 1415. The Duke was held prisoner for 25 years, in many places including the Tower of London, until a ransom of 400,000 gold crowns had been paid. Sir Richard was also responsible later for the arrest of the leader of the peasant rebellion of 1450, Jack Cade.

The present house stands on the moated site of the earlier ones and was built in brick by John Packer between 1652 and 1674, his father having bought the manor from the Waller family in 1608. It is an endearing house, soft and mellow with its years, unspoilt since the day it was built. It is H-plan with two storeys over a basement that rises sheer from the moat. It has large brick quoins and tall sunk panels in the chimney-stacks and over the front doors an especially attractive sandstone loggia, or gallery, supported by Ionic columns. Inside, use has been made of many of the old fittings from earlier houses — linen fold panelling with heads in the freize and arabesques. The stable block visible here is contemporary with the house and it has a particularly attractive lantern.

The gardens at Groombridge Place are said to have been laid out by the diarist John Evelyn who was an outstanding amateur landscape gardener and the first Englishman to write a learned treatise on the cultivation of trees. They are occasionally open to the public during the summer months.

The Pantiles, Royal Tunbridge Wells. Royal patronage of Tunbridge Wells began in 1606 when Lord North, mentor of James 1's son Prince Henry, took a cure in the area and was purged of his excesses by the iron-rich local waters and felt better for it. Thereafter the Court followed — Charles I's wife, Henrietta Maria, even camped on the common at one stage — and Tunbridge Wells became a fashionable watering place for London and society, a position it held until the passion for sea bathing and the seaside, notable Brighton, took over in the Regency period. It has prospered since then as a residential area. Whether the chalybeate waters were as much an attraction to its new inhabitants as its legacy of beautiful and dignified buildings is an open question. The Pantiles, seen here, was in the Wells' heyday called 'The Walks' and was first laid out in 1638. The colonnade was built in 1687 to shelter visitors from the rain as they walked to 'the waters' bubbling into two basins in the bath house. In 1697 the area of the springs was paved with pantiles at the instigation of Princess (later Queen) Anne. This present bath house (centre background) was built in 1804 and the canopy over the springs with its spindly columns and kiosk style roof is a typical Victorian addition dating from 1847. 'The Walks' became 'The Parade' in 1793 when they were paved with flagstones; they were renamed 'The Pantiles' in 1887 when part was repaved with the original pantiles some of which can still be seen near the springs.

Bayham Abbey, Lamberhurst. Between the latterday Bayham, a 19th century mansion built in 1870-72 by the architect David Brandon for the Marquess Camden, and the medieval Bayham Abbey, built between 1208 and 1211, runs the little River Teise which puts the house on the hill in Kent and the ruin in the valley in East Sussex.

The original Bayham Abbey was a Pro-menstratensian Community — known in England as the 'White Canons' because its members wore thick cloaks of undyed wool. It was the founding house of the order in England and there were 35 of them at the Dissolution when most, like Bayham, were reduced to ruins. What has survived is the gatehouse which now serves both abbeys, the buttressed wall of the nave of the abbey church, parts of the cloister and some storerooms. The whole, to some extent, serves the purpose of a picturesque romantic ruin of the age of Humphrey Repton who suggested the siting of the modern house in 1800.

The newer Bayham Abbey is in the Tudor style with a symmetrical front of local Wealden sandstone comprising two shaped gables. It looks over the ruin on one side and a lake on the other.

Not far from the ruins there once was an old furnace mill — the Weald was once a centre for iron-making — where were made half a mile of iron railings to go round St Paul's. The railings were taken down last century and sent to Canada but the ship was wrecked and only a few were saved.

22

Oasthouses at Hoathley, near Lamberhurst. The Wealden areas abound in hop-gardens and the culture of the hop has as much mysticism — and perhaps a little of the magic — in Kent as does the culture of the grape in the Bordeaux and Burgundy region of France. Hops grow in long aisles along wires mounted on hop poles eight foot high and ripen in August when they are picked, dried and sacked for delivery to the breweries. In earlier times the picking was done by hand and thousands of London's East Enders had a hardworking annual holiday in the hop gardens. Now picking is largely mechanical. The drying is done in the oast house which first came into being about 1575. 'Oast' means, however, the entire building, the store as well as the kiln. Originally oast houses were built with a raised middle bay standing over a charcoal furnace with storage either side for green or dried hops. At first the kilns were square but by the 19th century round kilns became the norm and it is these round conical hop kilns with their cowls and fly boards which are a distinctive feature of the Kent countryside.

Nineteenth century kilns had an inner wall supported by parabolic brickwork that created an internal chamber of diamond shaped section with the furnace at the bottom, the hop drying slatted floor at the widest point and the narrow neck of the kiln at the top to create the draught drawn in through vents at the base of the kiln and the inner brick ring. Hops took six to twenty hours to dry and hop drying was a highly skilled job. It also imparted to the Kent atmosphere an inimitable and unforgettable aroma. The cowl is traditionally painted white and usually had the farmer's emblem carved in silhouette on the flyboard. It moves with the wind to protect the kiln from the weather.

Oast houses are still used today but they are no longer built. Oil and gas firing, electric fans and roof louvres have now created an improved type of kiln which along with large open sheds to house the hop-picking machines are indicators of yet another industrial revolution in agriculture.

The Old Castle, Scotney, Lamberhurst. Old Scotney Castle is a picturesque ruin — and was meant to be. To achieve a beautiful landscape in the 18th century tradition of pictorial naturalism, William Hussey who built his new castle in 1837-44, pulled down part of the 17th century house that had earlier been built into the 14th century castle. To add even further to the scene he quarried the Wealden sandstone for his new house from immediately below the site. This ensured that the new building was in keeping with the old and the quarry itself, filled with shrubs and framed by a variety of trees, adds to the view from the terrace.

Scotney takes its name from the first owner of the manor, Walter de Scoteni who disappeared during the time of the Simon de Montfort troubles when the manor reverted to the Crown. In approximately 1378-80 Roger Ashburnham fortified his house probably as a result of the threat posed by the French who sacked Rye and Winchelsea in 1377. The defences comprise the moat which encircles two small islands, one of which, the larger, had curtain walls and four circular corner towers (one of these towers, the Ashburnham Tower, as can be seen still survives intact although its conical roof and lantern are a 17th century addition). Ashburnham's manor house, of the hall type, stood within the curtain walling with the entrance opposite the gatehouse. The house passed in 1411 to the Darell family whose home it remained for 350 years. It was improved and altered during the period until c1630 when it was completely rebuilt. The Darells became impoverished and sold Scotney in 1775. In 1778 it was purchased by Edward Hussey. His grandson inherited the Scotney estates c1828 and in 1836 decided to build the new Castle.

Under the stairs of the old castle is a hiding place leading to a skilfully concealed room under the roof. This was a genuine 'Priest's Hole' — the Darells were Roman Catholics — and a Jesuit, Father Richard Blount (1565-1638), hid in the castle for seven years from 1591. He was almost captured in 1598 but escaped with the help of Mrs Darell. He survived to become Provincial of the Jesuit Order in England in the more tolerant Stuart era.

Goudhurst. Goudhurst — the first syllable rhymes with 'loud' — lies on the Tunbridge Wells-Ashford road (A262) at the crest and slopes of a steep Wealden hill looking over miles of rich woodlands and apple and cherry orchards. It is said that 68 towers and spires can be seen on a clear day.

Both the church and the Star and Eagle Hotel opposite were built in the 15th century and Goudhurst has many fine timber-framed buildings covered with hung tiles and weatherboarding as this glimpse of the steep High Street reveals. The church is of particular interest; it was struck by lightning in 1637 — the spire burned and its bells melted. Its tower rebuilt in 1638-40 is a mixture of styles — classical and gothic of the kind found in contemporary churches in the City of London (St Katharine Cree, for example). It had its windows, tracery and glass replaced in the 19th century but lost its glass when a German landmine exploded near it in 1940. The church contains many monuments to the Culpeper family who lived in the area for many generations and played a large part in the history of both England and North America. Catherine Howard, King Henry VIII's fifth wife, was a Culpeper and her amorous adventures with her cousin Thomas Culpeper led them both to the scaffold. Later, Lord Culpeper was largely responsible for the process of bringing back Charles II at the end of Cromwell's Protectorate. Earlier another member of the family had helped to found Virginia and Carolina.

It was in Goudhurst where the idea that hops were grown in 'gardens' and not in fields originated. It is said that in 1341 the local vicar — who was paid by a tithe in kind on the produce of 'lambs, wool, cows, calves, chickens, pigs, ducks, apples, pears, onions and all other herbs sown in gardens . . .' — pleaded in the courts that hops too were grown in gardens and that he should receive a tithe on them. He lost his plea but the idea survived.

28

Cranbrook. Cranbrook is known as the 'capital' of the Kentish Weald and has a past going back to the early Middle Ages when it was the centre for iron-smelting. It was granted a market charter in 1290 but its real prosperity began in the 14th century when Edward III invited Flemish weavers from Louvain to settle in the little town. His purpose was to produce wool cloth in England instead of sending English wool abroad for processing. The idea was highly successful and 'Cranbrook Grey' became one of the best known Kentish broadcloths. The Flemish weavers built many of the attractive small houses in the town and gave generously to the local church of St Dunstan enlarging it to make it known as the 'Cathedral of the Weald'. They also once laid a mile of broadcloth for Queen Elizabeth to walk on — whether emulating or pre-empting Sir Walter Raleigh is not clear! Cranbrook is also famous for its windmill, seen here — the tallest mill in Kent and the largest working windmill in England. It dominates the town and is a full scale smock mill set on a brick base as tall as the mill itself. The windmill was built by Henry Dobell in 1814 and is still being worked — though not by the wind.

Cranbrook has two other claims to fame, one visible the other speculative. The first is the public school founded in 1520 with a foundation stone of School House laid by Queen Elizabeth I herself. The second is the belief that, in an unknown cottage near Cranbrook, Alexander Selkirk wrote *Robinson Crusoe*.

Sissinghurst Castle. Sissinghurst is not really a 'castle' — it did not acquire that title until the middle of the 18th century when French prisoners of war held there dubbed it 'chateau' which was then translated too literally into 'castle'. It is in fact the remains of a Tudor mansion saved in 1930 after decades of ruin and decay by the eminent writer and daughter of Knole, Vita Sackville-West and her husband, Harold Nicholson, the celebrated historian. They restored the buildings and created around them with great flair and imagination one of England's most outstanding gardens.

In the 12th century the site was called Saxinghorste and the family of that name built a moated manor there — the moat surviving in part to this day. A local family, the Bakers of Cranbrook, built a great Tudor house on the site of which only the entrance range survives together with the gatehouse and arch which the notorious Sir John Baker inserted in about 1535. Sir John Baker, a Catholic, has been held responsible for sending so many Protestants to the stake in Queen Mary's reign that he was known as 'Bloody Baker'. Some authorities, however, doubt the story. His son, Sir Richard Baker, demolished all except the entrance range in c1560-70 and built the tower and an Elizabethan courtyard house behind it. The Bakers backed the wrong side in ther Civil War losing their family fortune in the process and the decline of Sissinghurst began. It was leased to the Government in 1756 as a prison for French prisoners of war who promptly broke it up for firewood. In 1763 it was a wreck. Its decline continued and it became for 60 years a parish workhouse. Then in 1930 the pathetic ruin touched the heart of its rescuers who began the life-long task of restoration — they both died in the 1960s. The property now belongs to the National Trust and is open to the public from April to October.

The tower seen here was the gate tower of the Elizabethan house. It is built entirely of brick with quoins, windows and string courses rendered to resemble stone. The lefthand turret contains a spiral staircase while the righthand one forms small octagonal rooms on each floor. The room over the doorway was Vita Sackville-West's sitting room, and there she worked — where she 'could see without being seen'.

The gardens in their season are Sissinghurst's delight and at once a legacy and a memorial of the two artists who created them. The whole is made up of bewitching parts — Rose Garden, Lime Walk, Cottage Garden, Moat Walk, Nuttery, Herb Garden, Orchard — the most English of gardens in the garden of England.

Biddenden. The 'den' ending is familiar in this part of Kent and goes back to the days when the Weald was covered with forest. 'Den' meant a clearing in the forest used as a swine pasture — but who Bidda was remains a mystery. Not so much of a mystery, but nearly as old, is the village legend of the 'Maids of Biddenden' portrayed in the village sign in the foreground. Eliza and Mary Chalkhurst were twin sisters born joined together at the shoulders and hips. They lived for 34 years and then died within hours of each other. They left land in the village to provide loaves and cheese for the needy. This act is commemorated on Easter Monday each year at 10am by a dole of food for the poor of the parish. It includes cakes embossed with the figures of the Maids.

Even without its legend, Biddenden is a showplace. Even John Newman in the austere Pevsner series *Buildings of England* says of its village street seen here — 'very short and very perfect, at first sight seeming perfect to the verge of phoniness — but all is genuine . . .'

34

Tenterden. Perhaps the most delightful country town in Kent, Tenterden has known prosperity for centuries and its splendid houses show the work of builders in Elizabethan, Jacobean and, as here, Georgian styles — Victorian and modern too. Always a thriving agricultural centre it has also been, surprisingly to those who know only modern geography, a member of the Confederation of Cinque Ports with its port at Smallhythe, two miles to the south where Henry V once had men o' war built.

In medieval times — until 1284 — the sea came up in an inlet on either side of the Isle of Oxney. The great gale of 1284 caused the River Rother to change its course leaving the major port of Romney high and dry. After that time, in the reign of Edward, Tenterden benefited along with other Wealden villages from the arrival of Flemish weavers. It was also a centre for iron smelting.

Its church, St Mildred's, dates from 1180, carried a beacon that warned of the approach of the Spanish Armada and is connected by legend to the Goodwin Sands. It is said that they were once a fertile and settled island called Lomea but an abbot of St Augustine's diverted stones intended to fortify the sea wall to build the tower of Tenterden Church. The sea broke through the inadequate wall and submerged it. In fact there is no evidence that the island ever existed.

Tenterden's greatest son was William Caxton, the father of English printing, born here in 1422. He was the representative of the Merchant Venturers in the Low Countries and lived for over 30 years in Bruges and it was there that as a scholar, he learned the art of printing. He established a press at Westminster under the patronage of King Edward IV. Appropriately for a man of Kent, one of the earliest of his printed works was Chaucer's *Canterbury Tales*.

Smallhythe Place, near Tenterden. This splendid timber-framed house was built in the first half of the 16th century probably just after a great fire that destroyed Smallhythe in 1514. It was originally known as the Port House and was the harbour master's residence. When the sea receded it found a new role as 'The Farm'. Dame Ellen Terry, the celebrated actress, bought it in 1899 and lived there until her death in 1928. Her daughter, Miss Edith Craig, presented the property to the National Trust in 1939.

The house is of a type known as a 'continuous jetty' house because the first floor overhangs along the whole of the front elevation. Unlike the Kentish Wealden house, this type was built with two storeys throughout and with a chimney. The house is 'close-studded' (vertical wall-timbers close together) in the Kentish style and their oak has been left untreated. Internally the house retains much of its medieval layout which is intact with screens passage and inglenook fireplace.

Smallhythe Place is a memorial to Ellen Terry and contains many mementoes of her era. It is open to the public from March to

October.

Royal Military Canal, Ruckinge. The Royal Military Canal runs from the Kent coast at Seabrook just east of Hythe westwards to join the River Rother north of Rye. It was built in 1804-06 as part of the defences against an invasion by Napoleon. Its route lies just under the hills that surround Romney Marsh and it effectively turns the flatlands of the Marsh — an attractive landing area — into an island. How effective it might have been militarily was doubted even in Napoleon's time but its existing redoubts — there are embrasures every quarter of a mile or so — were reinforced with concrete pillboxes in 1940 when this again became an invasion coast. Ruckinge itself is on the north bank of the canal at roughly its mid-point. The canal has never been used for 'inland navigation' and nowadays as one writer put it 'is much favoured by anglers, moorhens, ducks and algae'.

Dungeness. The southernest point in Kent and growing southwards at a rate of about 18ft a year, Dungeness has been formed by the action of two contrary currents, one flowing north-eastwards on the flood, the other south-westwards on the ebb, along a coast of continuously shifting shingle. It is a desolate place largely given over to bird sanctuaries — particularly for migratory birds — under the control of the Royal Society for the Protection of Birds. It is also the site of two nuclear power stations, Dungeness 'A' and Dungeness 'B'.

Lympne Castle and Roman Fort. Lympne (pronounced 'Lim') was once the site of the Roman *Postus Lemanis* a fort on the 'Saxon Shore' — an invasion coast even then. It stands on the edge of the escarpment overlooking the eastern edge of Romney Marsh across the Royal Military Canal. The scattered stone ruins in the middle ground are those of Stutfall Castle (Stout Wall) which was one of four great Roman forts — the others are Reculver, Richborough and Dover — built about 280AD of coursed rubble with limestone facings. On the Wealden clay slope the massive structure with walls 20ft high and 14ft thick began to slide into the sea. It had to be abandoned about 370AD.

On top of the escarpment is Lympne Castle with a Norman church on its eastern side both of which had their origins in the 13th century. It is built of ragstone and the oldest part is the tower at the eastern end. The bow-fronted tower at the west end was added in the 15th century. Again this is one of Kent's 'courtesy castles' — largely a comfortable house in the hands of the archdeacons of Canterbury for most of its history until it was sold in 1860. It then became a ruin and it was restored in 1905 by F. J. Tennant who converted it into a modern private house. It is open to the public between July and September.

44

Martello Towers, Hythe. These Martello Towers were built in 1803-04 at the same time as the Royal Military Canal to provide defences against the threat of a French invasion. (They take their name from Martella in Corsica where a tower of similar design and structure had proved extremely difficult for the Royal Marines to capture in 1794.) They were brick built, about 30ft high, 22ft in diameter at the top and their walls are 5-8ft thick. They are designed to have a garrison of about 20-30 soldiers and to mount a 24-pounder gun. In the basement there was storage for water, food and ammunition. A chain of them ran — still runs — from the end of the Folkestone cliff along the coast to Eastbourne.

Folkestone Harbour. Although it had origins as a seaport in Roman times and was a 'limb' of the Cinque Ports under the control of Dover, modern Folkestone owes its present importance to the coming of the railways in the 1840s. What Defoe called 'a miserable fishing village' was transformed into a major packet station for the Continent and a fashionable seaside resort as well.

It stands on a sandstone shelf at the very eastern end of the Weald where the gault clay gives way to the chalk as is clearly visible here with the grassy East Cliff on the left and the more distant chalk Abbot's Cliff on the right. In the foreground is the yacht basin with the railway bridge behind it and beyond that the main harbour bounded by the East Pier and beyond the pier, Copt Point with its coastguard stations. At the foot of the cliffs on the left is The Stade running along the north edge of the harbour. It was rebuilt in 1935 with a row of brick and tile hung cottages on either side of the neo-Georgian Jubilee Inn. On the skyline is the westernmost of three Martello towers, the end of the chain around the uncliffed invasion coast. On the edge of the cliff beneath these towers are the lower courses of a Roman villa discovered in 1924 after a landslip. Mee suggests that it may have once been the home of the Roman 'Count of the Saxon Shore'.

Dover. A panoramic view of England's principal gateway, within its walls a microcosm of her island history since before the Romans came. The town takes its name from the little River Dour that cuts a steep valley through the chalk escarpment to the sea. The Romans built a lighthouse on Castle Hill, the Pharos, and constructed major roads, Watling Street, inland to Canterbury and London, northwards to their premier port at Richborough. In the 3rd and 4th centuries they added a fort as part of the defences of the 'Saxon Shore' and in 1064 King Harold began building on Castle Hill. After the battle of Hastings, William the Conqueror's first destination was Dover where he added to the work Harold had done — and secured a port in his rear. The main castle was built at the end of the 12th century and in 1216 withstood a siege by King John's rebellious barons. Dover saw the Spanish Armada pass through the Straits to its destruction off Calais. The castle was held by the Parliamentarians in the Civil War and Charles II landed here at the Restoration in 1660. In World War 1 it was the headquarters of the Dover patrol and columns in the town record 125,000 arrivals of ships and 120,000,000 landings of soldiers during the war. During World War 2 the port was frequently under attack from the air — the first raid of the Battle of Britain on 12 August 1940 fell on Dover — and more regularly from heavy artillery on the French coast.

The photograph looks over the Eastern docks with its vehicle ferries to the Admiralty Harbour — a basin enlarged early this century to take the whole of the British fleet. Beyond the harbour is the Commercial Harbour for passenger ferries and hovercraft. And behind that towers the bluff cliff that is near to every Englishman's heart. When we talk about the 'White Cliffs of Dover', most of us mean Shakespeare's Cliffe — named because of its imagined association with his play *King Lear* (Act IV, Scene 6) in which Edgar leads his blind father, the Earl of Gloucester, to the 'dread summit of this chalky bourn' where 'dizzy 'tis to cast one's eyes so low!'

In the centre along the shoreline is the great sweep of Waterloo Crescent, five-storeyed, stuccoed and painted white. It was built in 1834-8 and is in three parts of five, nineteen and five houses. On the skyline to the right there is just a glimpse of the Pharos and the tower of its adjacent church, St Mary in Castro.

St Margaret's at Cliffe. A village on the edge of a cove in the chalk cliffs of the South Foreland, St Margaret's suffered severely from German gunfire in World War 2. The Normans endowed it with a church on a noble scale — naturally St Margaret's — which was probably built c1140. Visible here on the skyline is the South Foreland lighthouse and to its left a weather boarded smock windmill built in 1929. The ship is the Townsend-Thoresen line car ferry plying between Dover and the Continent.

The Castle, Deal. Deal Castle is the middle one of three fortresses built by Henry VIII in 1539-40 to cover the anchorage between the Kentish shore and the Goodwin Sands known as The Downs. The other two were at Sandown and Walmer. They were designed as part of his scheme to combat a projected invasion by the King of France, backed by the Pope, to re-establish the Roman Church in England. They were never tested. English sea power proved a better deterrent.

The castle at Deal was in the hands of the Parliamentarians on the outbreak of the Civil War in 1642 but fell to the Royalists and was subsequently retaken. After the Restoration its garrison was reorganised under a Captain, a title that became purely honorary.

Sandwich. Now some two miles from the sea, Sandwich was for centuries a port of first importance. Its history began with the landings of the Romans in AD43. It was on the shore of what was then a large and sheltered bay with the Wantsum channel that then separated the Isle of Thanet from the mainland giving a short cut to the Thames estuary and London.

The Romans built their main supply depot at Richborough a mile and a half to the north but by the time they left a southward drift had built up a shingle bank and diverted the navigable channel to the south. The Saxons developed Sandwich and the marauding Danes attacked it; Canute and his father landed here with a large army in 1013. By the middle of the 15th century it was the main port of embarkation to the Continent and the most flourishing of the Cinque Ports. Then it seems, the current changed and built up an outer ridge of shingle that cut off Sandwich, in its turn, from the sea. The Wantsum itself remained navigable until about 1500 but silt finally closed it too. Sandwich ceased to be a port becoming instead, in Elizabeth's reign, a centre of the wool trade when Protestant refugees from France and the Netherlands settled in the town. Surprisingly little has happened since — and Sandwich is probably the quaintest town in Kent with a maze of little streets lined with houses from every period since the 14th century. The church of St Mary the Virgin is said to have stood on the site since the 7th century and was sacked and rebuilt several times. In 1667 its central tower collapsed and severely damaged the nave. It is now only a shell and is not used for services.

Ramsgate. The 'gate' here is not the harbour as one might expect but a break in the chalk cliffs where the old town was built. It has now spread over the tops of the cliffs on either side — West Cliff and East Cliff. Ramsgate in the Middle Ages was a minor Cinque Port, a 'limb' of Sandwich. In the 18th century after Sandwich silted up it became a port of refuge for ships seeking shelter when passing through the Downs — the gap between the coast and the dangerous Goodwin Sands. John Smeaton, the architect of the first Eddystone lighthouse, built the pier shielding the harbour of some 50 acres which on occasion is said to have held as many as 400 sail. Like so many seaside towns in Kent and Sussex it owes its modern development to the period of the Regency when sea bathing became fashionable. 'Ramsgate since the rage for sea bathing hath taken place, has had its share of visitants' wrote the 18th century writer Cozens, quoted by John Newman in the Pevsner series, *Buildings of England*.

Among such visitants was 'Prinny' himself. At the entrance to the East Pier is an obelisk to mark his departure from the port to Hanover in 1822 and his safe return — he was then, of course, King George IV. Another royal visitor was the young Princess Victoria.

These royal visitations explain the proliferation of royal titles in the town. An example here is the arcaded and medallioned Royal Parade ascending to the West Cliff with its Royal Crescent, 1826, of four-storeyed, pilastered and stuccoed houses and The Paragon, 1816, with its four-storeyed yellow brick terraces and splendid canopied balconies.

The celebrated neo-Gothic architect and enthusiast Augustus Pugin died in Ramsgate in 1852 and he built and paid for the Roman Catholic church of St Augustine which he considered his best work.

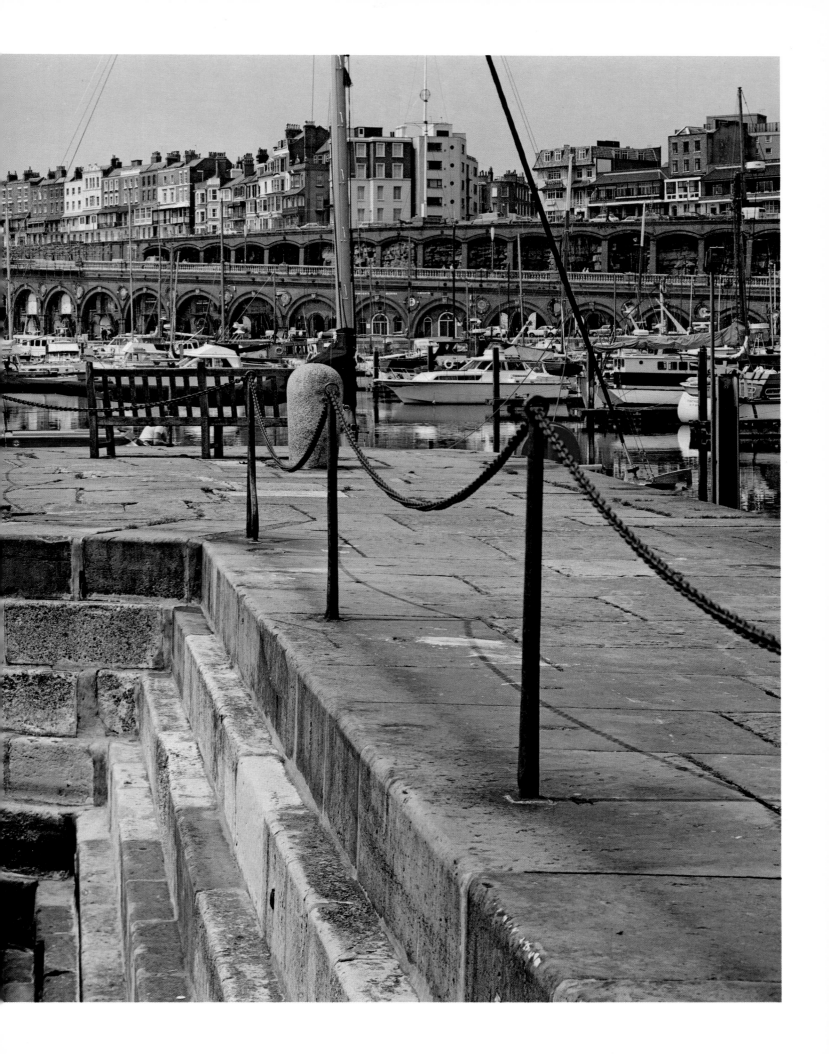

Reculver. The name Reculver is Old English for a 'great beak' or headland and the Romans established a fort here — Regulbium — to guard the entrance to the Wantsum channel that then ran through to their main port of Richborough. At that time the sea itself was a quarter of a mile off but eating away the coast at a rate of about a yard every year. In the 7th century St Augustine built the church here, St Peter and Paul, within the grounds of the Roman fort for his abbey at Canterbury. It comprised an aisleless nave with an apse. The twin towers were raised later — in the 12th century — it is said by an abbess of Davington to commemorate her sister's death and her own escape from drowning. They thus became known locally as 'The Sisters'.

By 1809, with the sea coming ever nearer, the vicar of the day, one C. C. Nailer, was persuaded to demolish most of it by his mother who 'fancied that the church was kept for a puppet show'. The stones were then used to build a new church at Hillsborough a village about a mile inland. But mariners sailing in and out of the Thames estuary made much use of the landmark of 'The Sisters' and accordingly the towers were restored in 1820 by Trinity House.

The Saxon origin of the surviving walls of the church are apparent from the square shape of the towers, the round headed west portal and the narrow slit-like windows. It is built of rubble stone and flint bonded at intervals by deep bands of Roman tiles.

Whitstable. Whitstable is on the north Kent coast at the mouth of the estuary of the Swale, the channel that connects the Medway to the Thames and makes Sheppey an island. It has been famous for its oysters for 2,000 years although whether Arthur Mee's suggestion that the promise of oysters and the prospect of pearls attracted Julius Caesar to Britain in the first place is true, we can only guess. What is not in doubt is the popularity of 'Whitstable natives' with all classes of successive generations. At the height of their prosperity, the area of the beds amounted to some 5,000 acres and they extended from some two miles offshore to over seven.

In 1830 Whitstable became the terminus of the first passenger railway designed to carry people from London who had been in the habit of sailing to Whitstable and going by coach to Canterbury. A Stephenson-built locomotive *Invicta*, now preserved in Dane John Gardens, Canterbury, pulled the inaugural train here in 1830. The railway bridge — built 1834 — is one of the earliest in the world and the tunnel through Tyler Hill was the first in Britain. The original Canterbury Rail Road Company scored another first, before it failed, in issuing the world's first railway season ticket. The railway was leased to the South Eastern Railway in 1844 and bought outright by them in 1853. Later the South Eastern as the South Eastern & Chatham merged with the Southern Railway at the grouping in 1923. The line itself was closed in 1931.

Westgate, Canterbury. *Ave Mater Anglia* (Hail Mother of England) is the city motto of this cradle of English Christianity and the seat of the Primate of All England, its archbishop. But Canterbury is more than a revered religious shrine with its memories of the martyrdom of Thomas à Becket. Even without its cathedral it would have been important as a garrison town and the major market place of the most fruitful of English counties. The Romans chose it as the nexus of their strategic road system in the southeast and stationed a garrison on the site. It guards the gap in the North Downs cut by the River Stour which in Roman times could have been as much as a mile wide. They cut roads from it to Richborough, their major port, to London, to Lympne and to Dover. They fortified the town and their town wall was followed almost exactly by the medieval defences. Westgate, seen here, stands close to the site of a Roman gateway called London Gate and is the only survivor of six original medieval gates. (The rest were pulled down in 1781.) It was built in 1375-81 and stands astride the London road on the banks of the narrow arm of the Stour. In the Middle Ages it would have had a drawbridge over the river. It certainly had a portcullis — the groove can still be seen — and all the other appurtenances of medieval fortification — battlements, arrow slits, and a narrow arch doorway with machicolations above it. The whole is built of massive squared ragstone blocks. Westgate was not much tested — it failed, however, to keep Wat Tyler out of the city — but it served as a useful prison from the 15th century to the 19th. It is now a museum with arms, armour, fetters and manacles and an old gallows.

Behind Westgate stands the church of Holy Cross built by Archbishop Sudbury (murdered by Wat Tyler and his mob in 1381) of knapped flint. It was heavily restored by the Victorians.

Greyfriars. At a point where the River Stour divides again to make an island within an island, stands the attractive ruin of the first Franciscan friary in England, founded in 1224 and moved to this site in 1267. The exact function of this ancient stone and flint building, 'patched with plenty of red brick' as John Newman says, is obscure. It may have been a dormitory — there is a contemporary fireplace on the first floor — or it may have been the warden's house. It has been altered many times since the friary was dissolved in 1538. Richard Lovelace (1618-58) the poet, lived here for some years and in the 18th century it was a meeting house for Presbyterians.

Christ Church Gate, Canterbury. This splendid prelude to Canterbury Cathedral and its precincts, Christ Church Gate dates from 1517. The heraldic shields, according to John Newman, commemorate Henry VIII's elder brother Prince Arthur who died in 1502. The massive carved wooden doors to both arches were broken up and burned during the Civil War. After the Restoration, Archbishop Juxon who, as Bishop of London, had given the last rites to King Charles I on the scaffold, replaced the doors. They bear his arms to this day. The octagonal turrets of the gateway were, it is said, removed in the 18th century because they stopped an alderman from seeing the

Cathedral clock to check his watch. The real explanation is probably that with the crumbling of the ragstone the turrets were becoming insecure and dangerous. They too were restored and the gateway itself was replaced in 1931-37 by the Friends of the Cathedral.

Canterbury Cathedral, Canterbury. This photograph of the floodlit cathedral is from the south with the buttressed walls of the south aisle in the foreground. The south transept is left of centre under the tower and the south-east transept beyond it.

The original cathedral, that founded by St Augustine in 597AD, is only a legend recorded by the Venerable Bede but Lanfranc, the first Norman archbishop, rebuilt a much larger church on the site. Of that building little now remains but the present nave and transepts stand on Lanfranc's foundations. There were further rebuildings in the Middle Ages — a new nave was erected in 1391-1405 — but these were not completed until 1468. The central tower 'Bell Harry', a noble example of the Perpendicular style, was built c1494; the south-west tower in c1430. The north-west tower, originally built by Lanfranc, was replaced in 1834 by a replica of the south-west tower. There have been major restorations since and inevitably work on the perishing stone is continuous. The cathedral is ninth in size among English cathedrals — York is larger in area, Winchester longer — and the nave is 188ft long, 72ft wide, 80ft high and the central tower is 235ft.

The story of the cathedral is no less and no more than the story of England in the millenium it has stood there. One incident, the murder of Thomas à Becket at the end of 1179, remains as a haunting legend to this day and the inspiration of pilgrims over the centuries. As T. S. Eliot puts it in his play *Murder in the Cathedral*:

For wherever a Saint has dwelt, wherever a martyr has given his blood for the blood of Christ
There is holy ground and the sanctity shall not depart from it
Though armies trample over it, though sightseers come with guide books looking over it.

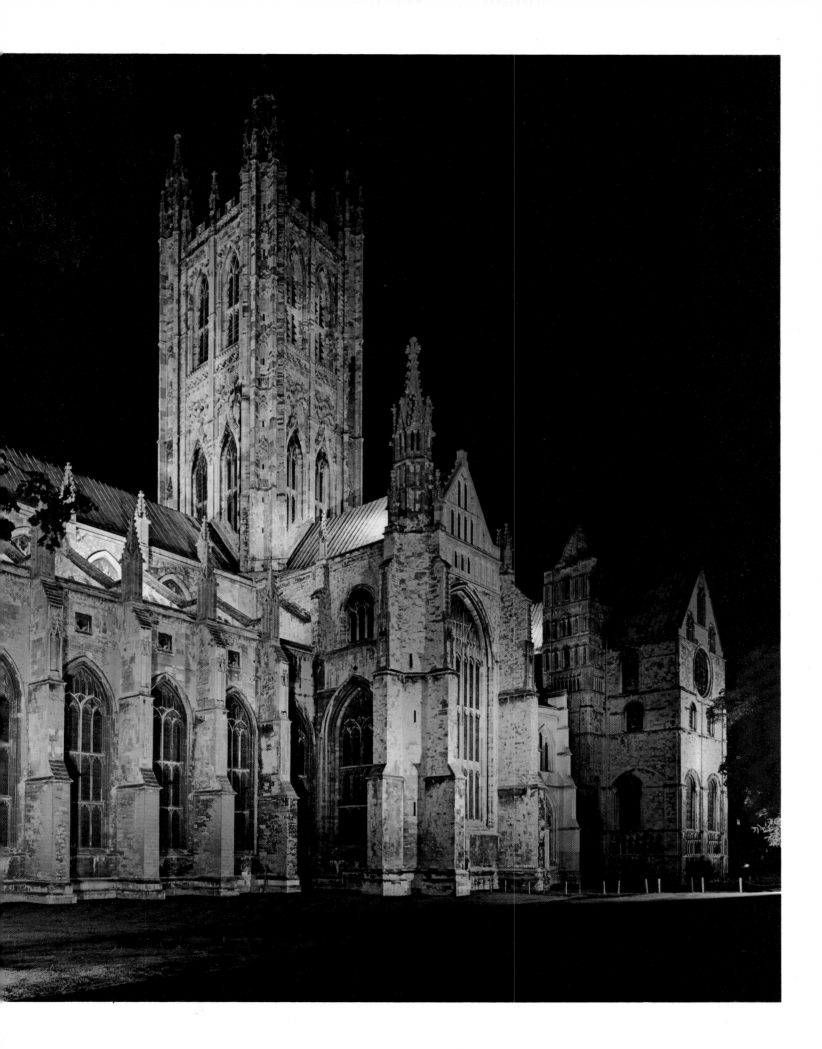

Sir John Boys' House, Canterbury. Sir John. Boys was an Elizabethan lawyer of a benevolent disposition who was 'Seneschal' (a sort of major-domo) to no less than five archbishops and has his statue in the cathedral as a reward. He died in 1612 but in 1595 he founded Jesus Hospital in Northgate, Canterbury. Fittingly perhaps, his house shown here in Palace Street is the King's School Shop. Lopsided and timber-framed, its plastered infill has at some time been made to look like rusticated stonework. The King's School was founded in 1541 by Henry VIII as a grammar school for about 50 boys. It followed directly from a monastic foundation of the 7th century and King Henry made the last master of the monastic school the first master of King's School and thus the school itself became effectively the oldest in the country. It now has about 800 boys. Among its former pupils are Christopher Marlowe (1564-93) the poet and dramatist; William Harvey (1578-1657) who discovered the circulation of the blood; and in more recent times, W. Somerset Maugham the novelist. Field Marshal Montgomery had one term in the junior school.

72

Wye Downs. This ridge in the North Downs
rising away from the valley cut by the Stour
takes its name from the ancient little town
of Wye which was a royal manor before the
Norman conquest. Parts of the North
Downs with crisp dry turf and open skies
are well suited as sheep pastures and Wye
itself is the site of Wye College, the
agricultural college of London University
with an international reputation. Appropriately, it has a department devoted to hop
research and horticulture.

The Pilgrims' Way to Canterbury turns
north-eastward up the Stour valley to
Canterbury but the North Downs Way,
another ancient trackway, continues close
to this point on its way along the edge of
the escarpment to Folkestone. This photograph was taken close to the nature reserve
on the edge of Wye Downs — the Wye &
Crundale Nature Reserve which is 250
acres in extent. It was established by the
Nature Conservancy to preserve a typical
area of chalk down and woodland with its
plants and wild life in a natural state.

Eastwell Park with its lake sits on the Pilgrims' Way on the escarpment of the North Downs just before the Way turns north-east towards Canterbury. The main house is relatively modern but the house seen here — Lake House, until recently derelict and overgrown — is now believed to date from the 13th century. An unusually large stone house with an upper hall, most of its open windows are 19th century but some of the blocked ones appear original.

At Eastwell too, there is a legend (Mee tells it best) of how an early medieval owner, Sir Thomas Moyle, was fascinated to discover that one of the elderly workmen building his house could read Latin. His name was Richard and further investigation revealed that he was the son of Richard III, England's last Plantagenet king killed at Bosworth in 1485. He had seen his father last on the eve of the battle and on the king's instructions, the battle lost, he had fled eastwards and merged his identity into that of a common labourer — and survived. He died in 1550 and his tomb is said to be in Eastwell church, alas now ruined since it was damaged by a bomb in World War 2.

Harefield Farm, Selling. A hop-garden in early spring — the first shoots begin the long climb up the wires set out for them. The heavy fertiliser layer is customary — at one time feathers and waste shoddy from Yorkshire woollen mills used to be spread over the roots. Traditionally the cats' cradle of wires was tended by men on stilts — or with specially made ladders — and the women 'twiddled' the hop shoots on to the wires. Hops need protection from strong winds especially when they 'hang hale and good' from the top lattice of wires. The gusts and eddies do the damage then, and the slatted screen in the foreground is intended to smooth out the wind stream.

Hops were first introduced into Kent in the 16th century. The area devoted to hops is declining partly as a result of imported hops, partly because of higher yields. There are many varieties suited to the wide range of soils found in the county. In the background are the typical cowled conical drying kilns.

78

Cherry Orchard, near Faversham. This cherry orchard lies between the hamlets of Throwley and Eastbury on the edge of the main orchard belt in North Kent which runs between Sittingbourne and Faversham. The soils in the area are light and warm up quickly in spring and summer and drain easily and the area has excellent communication with the great London markets along the M2. Sheep are grazed in the orchards early in the year but removed when the fruit are well-grown. The sheep here appear to be of the Kent and Romney Marsh breed — renowned across the world for the fine quality of their wool.

In spring the countryside in these parts is blanketed with blossom. The cultivation of cherries in Kent has, however, suffered in recent years from imports, especially from Italy. The chief varieties — grown on ancient trees — are Early Ruers, Napoleon and Noir de Gubin.

Faversham Creek. The north coast of Kent is heavily indented with muddy tidal inlets like the one shown here and they have helped over the centuries to bring prosperity to several small country towns. Faversham was first established where the Roman Watling Street from Canterbury to London crossed this inlet from the Swale which runs into the Thames estuary. As the creek silted up, so the town moved closer to the sea.

Faversham in the Middle Ages enjoyed the privileges and status of being a corporate member of the Cinque Ports in association with Dover. It received its charter and mayor in 1225. Its most notable contribution to history came, however, in 1688 when its fishermen captured James II and brought him back to the port when the smack in which he was escaping to France ran ashore at the mouth of the Swale. In the 18th century it enjoyed an affluent trade in the smuggling of French brandy and wine.

Nowadays it has breweries, brickworks and flour mills and imports a great deal of timber. But as can be seen from the almost unreadable sign on the warehouse, the trade in fertilisers seems to have replaced that in oysters.

The Guildhall, Faversham. But Faversham has another role — as a market town in the centre of the richest fruit growing area in Kent. The Guildhall was originally built as a market hall in 1574 but converted into a Guildhall in 1604. The arcades are octagonal and made of timber and divide the area below the Guildhall into two. The upper part of the building was rebuilt in the early 19th century as the Venetian window partly visible here demonstrates. The cheerful pump in the foreground probably dates from the same time.

With its long history, Faversham has a wealth of fascinating small houses and interesting corners — note, for example, the medieval pointed stone doorway on the right.

84

Charing. Another village at the foot of the North Downs and astride the Pilgrims' Way is Charing, once an important halt for pilgrims on their way to Canterbury. The archbishop had a palace here — the ruins are visible to the left of the church — and Henry VIII stayed there on his way to the Field of the Cloth of Gold. At the Dissolution in 1538 Cranmer resigned the palace to the king but it was allowed to fall into decay. It is now part of a farm.

What can be seen in the photograph is the ruin of the gatehouse with its two arches — the main and the subsidiary for foot travellers. The remnants of a fireplace are visible in the wall to the right of the arch. Inside the arch the buildings are grouped irregularly around a courtyard which now does duty as a farmyard. The walling is of knapped flint.

The church is also of special interest and, Newman says, is characteristically Kentish. Built of ragstone ashlar between c1479 and 1537, its tower in the Kentish Perpendicular style is particularly fine. Notice the turret at the south-east corner. The area in front of the church was once the village marketplace.

Boughton Malherbe, Charing. There are several 'Boughtons' in Kent. The name derives from 'the town of the beeches' reflecting the frequent stands of fine beech trees found along the drier uplands of Kent — just as apple orchards tend to be. 'Malherbe' is a family name and uncomplimentary — 'evil weed'. The manor here was once the property of the Wotton family who had 'herbal' Norman origins. One of the Wottons was the poet Sir Henry — died 1639 — who was responsible for that diplomatic chestnut that 'an ambassador is an honest man sent to lie abroad for the good of his country'. He also wrote one of the most touching of epitaphs upon the grave of the wife of his friend:

He first deceased; she for a little tried
To live without him: liked it not and died.

Headcorn Manor, Headcorn. Headcorn Manor is a restored Wealden house standing almost in the churchyard as the old tombstones indicate. It was originally built as a parsonage in 1516. This style of house — built for people in the yeoman farmer class to which medieval clerics might aspire — is found all over the south-eastern counties but is most numerous in the Weald of Kent and Sussex. Its characteristics are clearly visible in the house in the photograph — a rectangular ground plan with a central hall and wings with jettied (over-hanging) upper storeys all under a single-hipped roof. The central hall is usually open to the roof and is recessed beneath deep eaves supported by curved braces. The 'wings' have service rooms on the ground floor of one end, private rooms at the other, chambers above both. Features of particular interest in this Wealden house are the two storey oriel window lighting the hall, the single oriel windows in the upper storeys of the jettied wings, the closed spaced studding and the four-centre doorway.

Dragon House, Smarden. Another of the 'dens' of the Kentish Weald, Smarden stands on the River Boult, one of the tributaries of the Medway. Like Tenterden and Cranbrook it was licensed as a market town by Edward III in 1332 but never grew beyond a village. Its church of St Michael — the tower visible here in the background — was built in anticipation of better things. The width and height of its aiseless nave with the unusual scissor-beam room and built all of stone at one go have earned it the name of 'the Barn of Kent'. The Perpendicular west tower has particularly bold battlements and a many-sided north-east turret.

The Dragon House is so-called because of the dragon motif in the frieze beneath the overhanging upper storey. It probably dates from the 17th century.

Teston, River Medway. This fine Tudor rag-stone bridge carries the B2163 across the Medway to join the A26. Only the three centre arches are medieval, the others were built in matching style in the 19th century. Teston, through Barham Court — close to where this photograph was taken — is associated with the early days of the movement to abolish slavery. James Ramsay, a naval chaplain to Admiral Middleton, who owned Barham Court, retired to the living at Barham. Appalled by what he had seen of the slave trade in the West Indies he began in 1781 the campaign that eventually led to its abolition. He is said to have met William Wilberforce at Barham Court in 1783.

The Archbishop's Palace, Maidstone. Like so many desirable sites in Kent, Maidstone was once the property of the Archbishop of Canterbury who established a residence here in King John's reign and kept it until the Dissolution.

Maidstone was not incorporated until 1549 and then lost its charter in 1554 for supporting Wyatt's rebellion against Mary Tudor's Spanish marriage. It was restored by Queen Elizabeth in 1559 and its central position meant that the county administration was steadily concentrated there. In 1648 the Kentish Royalists were halted by Fairfax after a brief siege and in the 19th century, it became Disraeli's first seat.

The Archbishop's Palace seen here stands close to All Saints Church — a spacious collegiate church built in 1395 by Archbishop Courtenay. The tower in the Kentish style with its typical stair turret is rather undersized for the unusually wide nave and aisles — said to be able to seat 1,500 people. (Fairfax found it a commodious gaol for his Royalist prisoners.)

To the right of the church is the building which was once the College of Secular Canons, completed in 1397 with an embattled gatehouse. The Archbishop's Palace, north-west of the church, is usually called 'Old Palace'; it was built originally in 1349-66 but altered in 1486-1500 by a later archbishop. The river front seen here was restored in 1909 and all its windows date from that period. It has a panelled banqueting hall, a fine 16th century staircase and some quaint carvings. At one time it belonged to the Astley family; one of them, Sir Jacob Astley who fought for the King at Newbury, was the author of the prayer:

Lord, I shall be very busy this day,
I may forget Thee, but do not Thou forget me.

Aylesford. Said to have been the site of the great battle between Hengist and Horsa and the Ancient Britons under Vortigern that established the English in the land in 449AD, Aylesford used to command the lowest ford across the Medway. It was also the crossing point for the Pilgrims' Way to Canterbury. The bridge itself is made of rag-stone and dates from the 14th century although the widened central arch was a later alteration to cope with river traffic. Notice the neat little refuges projecting over the buttresses.

Local legend has it that Kits Coty — a great chamber made of huge stones weighing several tons each — was once the tomb of Vortigern who died in personal combat with Horsa. It is also said that it is possible on dark nights to see a spectral action replay of that particular encounter — but in total silence.

The Keep, Rochester. Dominating the river, the town and the cathedral, Rochester's castle guards Watling Street at its most vulnerable point on the route from Dover to London — the lowest point at which the Medway could be bridged. The keep is one of the finest pieces of Norman military architecture in England and the castle was one of the first to be built after the Conquest, parts dating from 1077. The keep itself was built between 1127 and 1139 by the then Archbishop of Canterbury. It is also the tallest of the tower keeps — 125ft to the turret tops. Its walls are between seven and ten feet thick, made of ragstone rubble.

Rochester Castle was successfully attacked by King John in 1215 in his battles with his barons when his engineers undermined the south-east turret. (This was before the introduction of 'machicolation' — slots for dropping boiling oil and molten lead on people who came too close to the walls.) It later withstood a siege by Simon de Montfort in 1264 but fell again to Wat Tyler and his mob in 1381. It was dismantled in the early part of the 18th century and its timbers were used to build a brewery.

Rochester is the second cathedral city of Kent and is famous for its association with Charles Dickens who spent his childhood in nearby Chatham. Rochester is mentioned in several of his books — *Pickwick Papers, Great Expectations* — and a number of old houses in the town can be recognised from his descriptions.

Upnor, River Medway. Upnor commands the entrance to Chatham Reach and the castle was built in 1559-67 to guard the new dockyards and naval stores at Chatham. It was of a new design with a low gun platform equipped with heavy guns in a triangular bastion in front of the main building. As the threat from the Armada increased, a massive iron chain was stretched across the river below Upnor.

The castle was further improved in the 17th century but it failed to prevent the Dutch fleet under de Ruyter setting fire to the British fleet in Chatham in 1667. After that disgraceful event — John Evelyn, the diarist, called it 'as dreadful a spectacle as ever any Englishmen saw and a dishonour never to be wiped off' — the castle was further enlarged. It later became an armoury and powder store.

In the 19th century the prison hulks that Charles Dickens writes about in *Great Expectations* were moored off Upnor. Later still, the training ship *Arethusa* was anchored just offshore from where this photograph was taken.

The castle was bombed in 1941; in 1961 it became an official National Monument and is open to the public.

View over the Halston Marshes, Cooling. The peninsula between the estuary of the Medway and the Thames is called the 'Hundred at Hoo' with, at its eastern end, the Isle of Grain. We are looking northwards here from the side of the road between Cooling and High Halstow across the Hadlow marshes, the Thames fairway and on to the large oil port and refinery at Thameshaven on the Essex coast. It is a bleak area — even on a sunny day as in the photograph — and it is, again, part of the background against which Dickens set *Great Expectations*. He describes it through the eyes of his boy hero, Pip, thus: '. . . and that the dark wilderness beyond the churchyard, intersected with dykes and mounds and gates, with scattered cattle feeding on it, was the marshes: and that the lower leaden line beyond was the river; and that the distant savage lair from which the wind was rushing, was the sea . . .'

In the middle ground is the Northward Hill nature reserve, noted for its heronry.

104

Meopham (pronounced 'Mep'am') is one of the first and last villages in Kent depending upon whether one is entering or leaving the great suburban sprawl of south-east London. It was the birthplace of John Tradescant (1608-62) who with his father was gardener to Charles I and founder of the first natural history collection in England — the Ashmolean in Oxford. The Tradescants travelled to America and Australia and introduced many plants to England, acacia, plane, lilac — and, of course, that much-loved indoor plant Tradescantia, or Spider-wort.

Meopham Green seen here is noted for its village cricket ground and its windmill. The latter, hexagonal on a hexagonal base, is a smock mill with black weatherboarding and a boat-shaped cap. It was built in 1801 as a demonstration mill. Four famous Kent and Surrey players are portrayed on the sign of the Cricketers' Inn.

106

Eynsford. The ancient village of Eynsford is a crossing place of the River Darent which winds its way from the Weald to the Thames. The ford dates back to Roman times and is still in use; the bridge to its right was built in the 17th century. The Normans built a castle here in the 11th century but it was occupied for only a brief period and has stood empty and ruined since the days of Thomas à Becket. The first owner, Lord of the Manor of Eynsford William Fitzralph, quarrelled with Becket who excommunicated him. Fitzralph complained to his friend King Henry I and contributed to the chain of events that led to Becket's murder in Canterbury cathedral in 1170. In remorse Fitzralph gave up his castle and went into a monastery.

Across the road is the Plough Inn, with its timber-framed gable. The close studding — vertical timbers close together — is typical of this type of building in the 16th century. Note also the frilly bargeboard, the overhanging jetty, the small windows, the concave lozenge in the gable, and the multi-flued chimney stack with its decorative shape and oversailing brick courses.

Mill House, Farningham. Farningham was a stopping place on the 18th century coach road from London to Dover. it is now by-passed by both the A20 and the M20 and its centre remains a handsome 18th century village with manor house, church, farm and mill all in a row. The notoriously irascible Captain Bligh of the *Bounty* spent his declining years — he died in 1817 an Admiral — in the manor house after his exciting and adventurous life. As well as the celebrated Mutiny, he took part in a voyage around the world with Captain Cook at the age of 20 — no doubt where he learned his skill as a navigator. He later saw war service under Nelson at Copenhagen.

The church, St Peter and St Paul, is 13th century in origin and built of flint. In its churchyard is the mausoleum of Thomas Nash, who died in 1778, believed to have been an early work of his nephew, the celebrated architect John Nash, whose works include Marble Arch, Buckingham Palace and the Royal Pavilion, Brighton. Of more traditional design are the watermill, mill house, grain store and cottages seen here. the house is three bays and 18th century in origin of red and grey brick. The white weatherboarding of the mill itself has been the hallmark of Kent ever since soft-wood was imported through Deal in the 18th century.

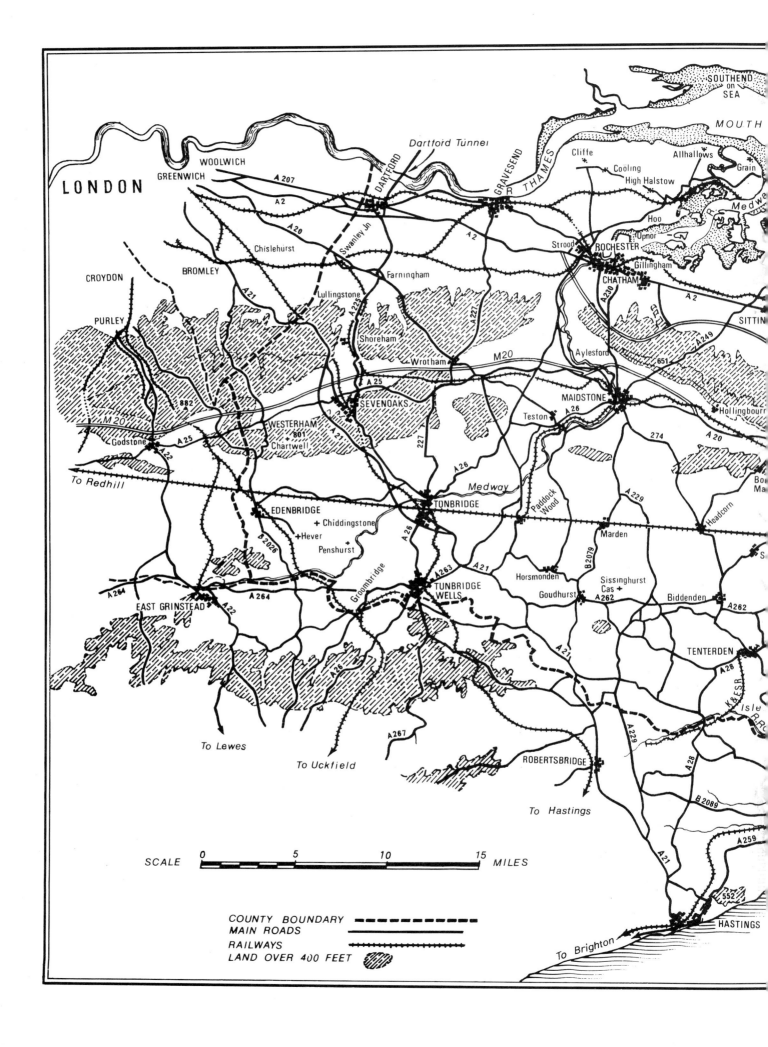

LONDON

SOUTHEND on SEA

MOUTH

R THAMES

Dartford Tunnel

WOOLWICH

GREENWICH

A 207

A 2

A 20

Chislehurst

Swanley Jn

DARTFORD

GRAVESEND

Cliffe

Cooling

High Halstow

Allhallows

Grain

Medway

Hoo

Upnor

CROYDON

BROMLEY

A 21

Farningham

A 2

Strood

ROCHESTER

Gillingham

CHATHAM

A 2

PURLEY

Lullingstone

A 225

A 227

Shoreham

A 230

SITTIN

882

M 20

Wrotham

M 20

Aylesford

651

A 249

SEVENOAKS

A 25

MAIDSTONE

WESTERHAM

801

Chartwell

A 21

227

Teston

A 26

Hollingbourr

M 20

A 25

274

A 20

Godstone

A 22

To Redhill

A 26

Medway

Paddock
Wood

A 229

Bo
Ma

EDENBRIDGE

+ Chiddingstone

+Hever

Penshurst

B 2026

TONBRIDGE

A 26

Marden

B 2079

Headcorn

S

Groombridge

A 263

A 21

Horsmonden

Sissinghurst
Cas +

A 264

A 264

A 22

TUNBRIDGE
WELLS

Goudhurst

A 262

Biddenden

A 262

EAST GRINSTEAD

A 26

A 21

TENTERDEN

A 28

K & E S R

Isle
R

To Lewes

A 267

A 28

To Uckfield

ROBERTSBRIDGE

A 229

B 2089

To Hastings

A 21

A 259

SCALE   0   5   10   15   MILES

552

COUNTY BOUNDARY – – – – –
MAIN ROADS ————
RAILWAYS ┼┼┼┼┼┼┼┼┼┼
LAND OVER 400 FEET

HASTINGS

To Brighton